The Bose Family of Faridpur

Siva Prasad Bose and Joy Bose

Published by Joy Bose, 2022.

The Bose Family of Faridpur

By Siva Prasad Bose and Joy Bose

Published by Joy Bose

Copyright © 2022 Siva Prasad Bose

Contents

Dedication

This book is dedicated to all branches of the Bose family settled in different parts of the world.

Preface

This book presents the history of a Bengali family from Ulpur village in Faridpur in East Bengal, which is now part of Bangladesh. This is the story of our family, known as the Basu Roy Chowdhury family, or more simply the Bose family.

Our ancestors had been granted land deeds from the Mughal emperor and became jagirdars in Ulpur in Faridpur district. Over time, our family established a large Zamindari Bari (landlord's estate), and this survived through the British era as well. During partition of India in 1947, most of the family being Bengali Hindus, lost their lands and fled west to India, although a few remained in Ulpur. A temple to Goddess Kali and other smaller temples still exist on the estate.

This book is a collection of historical facts, family memories, and heritage information. We discuss the history of the Bose family and the surviving buildings in Ulpur. We also go through the settling of a branch of the Bose family in New Delhi and the institutions for Bengalis available in New Delhi.

This book is a summary of our family and its history. We hope it will be a valuable resource for people interested in Indian family histories.

Acknowledgements

In preparing this book, we are very thankful to several resources available online and in research papers about the history of the Bose or Basu Roy Chowdhury family of Ulpur.

Some of the sources consulted are as follows:

- Ulpur Sammilani 21/1, Central Park, Flat B-2, Kolkata 700 032 Tel: 2425 4348. Website: http://www.ulpur.org/home/
- Empire's Last Casualty by Sabyasachi Ghosh Dastidar, Feb 2008. URL: http://empireslastcasualty.blogspot.com/2008/02/ ulpur-gopalganj-faridpur-district.html by Sabyasachi Ghosh Dastidar
- Wikipedia articles on Ulpur and Bengali Kayasthas. URL: https://en.wikipedia.org/wiki/Ulpur
- Offroad Bangladesh. Ulpur Zamindar Bari. URL: http://offroadbangladesh.com/places/ulpur-zamindar-bari/
- Daily Asian Age, July 2017. The historical place at Gopalganj. URL: https://dailyasianage.com/news/70639/the-historical-place-at-gopalganj
- The Financial Express, Oct 13 2020. Ulpur Zamindar House in Gopalganj in shabby state. URL: https://thefinancialexpress.com.bd/national/ulpur-zamindar-house-in-gopalganj-in-shabby-state-

1602589494
- Google maps. Maps Data @ Google 2022

Timeline of the Bose Family

The following timeline summarizes the key events in the history of the Basu Roy Chowdhury family of Ulpur, from their earliest recorded origins to the present day.

Date / Period	Event
~11th century AD	Dasarath Basu arrives in Bengal's Rarh region. His descendants become the founders of the Basu Roy Chowdhury lineage.
~16th century	Raghunandan Basu receives the Jagir/Zamindari of Ulpur (Shahpur) from Mughal Emperor Jahangir as a do hazari (2,000 horsemen) jagir.
17th century	Family adopts the title Thakur; later receives the Mughal title Chowdhury. Ulpur becomes the established central seat of the Shahpur Pargana.
Early 1900s	Zamindar Pritish Chandra Roy Chowdhury builds the main Ulpur Zamindari Bari complex on 200 acres of land. The estate at its height includes over 100 buildings.
1905	First Partition of Bengal by Lord Curzon divides Bengal into East and West. Reversed in 1911.
1931	Shahpur Pargana has a recorded population of 30,200 across 27 maujas, with Ulpur as the central seat of the Zamindari.
1933	Sarbari Roy Chowdhury, notable sculptor of the Basu Roy Chowdhury family, born in Ulpur.
1947	Second Partition of Bengal. Faridpur, including Ulpur, goes to East Pakistan. The Bose family, being Hindu Kayasthas, lose their ancestral lands and migrate to India. Most branches settle in Kolkata; one branch settles in Delhi.
Late 1940s	The Delhi branch of the Bose family settles first in Gandha Nala market near Mori Gate, then moves to Kashmere Gate in Old Delhi. Boys attend Bengali Boys Senior Secondary School.
1950s–60s	Lipika Bose, elder sister, works as an English lecturer commuting Delhi–Meerut to fund her brothers' education. The family lives as a joint family at Bedi Bhavan, Kashmere Gate.

1954	East Bengal Displaced Persons (EBDP) Association formed in Delhi to support partition refugees.
1971	Bangladesh Liberation War. East Pakistan becomes Bangladesh. Subrata Roy Chowdhury of the Ulpur family helps draft the proclamation of independence of Bangladesh.
1984	Greater Faridpur district split into five districts; Ulpur's area now part of Gopalganj district, Bangladesh.
~1968–2000s	Delhi branch of the Bose family obtains a plot in the new Bengali colony (later named Chittaranjan Park, or CR Park). Lipika Bose builds a three-storey house there from her own savings.
2012	Sarbari Roy Chowdhury, renowned sculptor and family member, passes away.
2015	Lipika Bose passes away, surrounded by her extended family, having ensured the stability and education of all three brothers and the wider family.
2022	One of the authors visits Ulpur Zomidar Bari in August 2022. A new museum complex dedicated to Bangabandhu Sheikh Mujibur Rahman is built on the estate grounds. This book is published.

Chapter 1: Researching Our Bose Family

In this chapter, we cover our motivation to research about the origins of our Bose family.

1.1 Research from Spoken Memories

We always knew our origins were from Faridpur district in East Bengal, but did not have much more data. There were not many written records except a land deed that our grandfather brought when he escaped to India, and which helped him to get an equivalent piece of land in New Delhi thanks to the kindness of the Indian government at that time.

Whenever we used to ask our elders, the elder aunt, Boro Pishi, used to say that we came from Ulpur village but did not remember much further details. Also, most of the elders who remembered have passed away. Therefore, our main source of information remains online sources, books, conversations with other people and visiting the ancestral places.

1.2 Research from Internet

Searching the internet, we found some very helpful resources and information about Ulpur and our family, particularly on the Wikipedia page for Ulpur and on the ulpur.org website. Notably, the famous Indian novelist Amitav Ghosh, whose mother Anjali Basu Roy Chowdhury was from the same Ulpur family, also visited the Zamindar Bari in recent years, drawing wider attention to the site.

Despite these discoveries, documented information remains sparse. This inspired us to write this book and bring together the collected information in one place.

1.3 Personal Visit by the Author to Our Ancestral Home in Ulpur

Another source of information is a personal visit by one of the authors to Ulpur Zomidar Bari site, by taking a taxi along with tour guide from Dhaka.

The author visited Ulpur village and zomidar bari in August 2022 in a day trip. It is possible to visit Ulpur in a day trip thanks to the newly opened expressway on Padma River, which cuts the 180-200 km journey time to around 3-4 hours each way.

1.4 Bose Family After Partition

Upon partition, several branches of the Bose family settled in different parts of India and abroad, many in Kolkata. Our family moved and settled down in Kashmere Gate in Delhi, in a rented place called Bedi Bhavan which was close to the Delhi Engineering College campus in Kashmere gate. After a few decades around 2000s, our family then moved to Chittaranjan Park in Delhi.

This book is a collation of materials collected from various sources, as well as our own memories concerning our family.

Chapter 2: Origins of Bose or Basu Roy Chowdhury Family

In this chapter, we briefly look at the origins of the Bose family in Bengal.

2.1 Origin of the Bengali people

Bengalis are the people who speak the Bangla language and its dialects, and are inhabitants of eastern India and Bangladesh. Predominantly of Indo-Aryan stock, they form the third largest ethnic group in the world after the Han Chinese and Arabs. The Bangla language is the sixth most widely spoken language in the world. Bengalis follow Hinduism, Islam, and a variety of other religions, including Buddhism.

Vanga and Gauda are old names for different Bengali kingdoms in medieval times. After the rule of the Pala and Sena dynasties, the area known as Bengal today was unified into one kingdom by King Shamsuddin Iliyas Shah in the 14th century, and the modern form of the Bangla language developed around the same time.

The Charyapada or Charyagiti — a collection of poems and songs from the 9th to 11th centuries AD, composed by various Buddhist siddha mystics such as Saraha — is considered one of the oldest texts of Bengali literature. These songs offer a glimpse into Bengali society of that era and attest to the antiquity of the language. The Bhakti movement led by Chaitanya Mahaprabhu arose in Bengal in the 15th century, giving a new spiritual impetus to the region. During the period of British rule, Bengal became the centre of the Indian renaissance of the 18th and 19th centuries, producing luminaries such as Rabindranath Tagore, the Nobel Prize-winning poet, and the scientists Jagadish Chandra Bose and Satyendra Nath Bose.

Faridpur district, from which our family hails, sits in the fertile floodplain of the Padma river (the lower Ganges). The district's soil is highly fertile, and its rivers — including the Kumar, Arial Khan, Gorai, Chandana, and Modhumoti — have sustained a rich agricultural and cultural life for centuries. The district has a distinguished history as one of the most politically active regions of the Bengal Presidency during the British Raj, producing several nationalist leaders.

2.2 Origins of the Bengali kayasthas to which Bose family belong

The kayasthas, a sub caste of Hinduism, are believed to have emerged around the Gupta period of 5th - 6th century AD.

As per legend, the kayasthas migrated to Bengal from Kannauj in North India along with a few Brahmins, at the invitation of king Adisur around the 10th century AD (Luca et al, 2017). The five kayastha families who migrated to Bengal got the surnames Bose, Ghosh, Mitra, Guha and Dutta.

Some Bengali historians believe the Adisur legend refers to the Sena king of Bengal Hemanta Sen. According to historian Dr Niharranjan Ray, in his book history of Bengal (Banglar itihas), all Sena rulers of Bengal also adopted a derivative of the title Sur.

Adisur could be one of the titles taken by Hemanta Sen, the Sena king of Bengal and grandfather of Ballal Sen who started the Kulin system in Bengal.

The paper by Luca et al (2017) also shows the genealogical links of Bengali kayasthas with other communities in India. Some scholars have postulated that the kayastha community in Bengal merged with different castes over time. Eventually, this group of people formed an elite group in Bengali society after the brahmins.

2.3 Origins of the Surname Bose or Basu

Bose is a common Indian surname among Bengali Hindus from the Kayastha caste. Famous Indian people with this surname include the freedom fighter Subash Chandra Bose and the scientist Jagadish Chandra Bose.

From the Wikipedia article on Bose surname:

Bose, Basu, Bosu, Boshu or Bosh (Bengali: ◇◇◇, romanized: Bôsu, Bengali pronunciation: [boʃu]) is a surname found amongst upper caste Bengali Hindus. It stems from Sanskrit ◇◇◇◇ (Vāsu, a name of Viṣṇu meaning 'dwelling in all beings').

Boses belong to Kayastha caste in Bengal. The Bengali Kayasthas evolved between the 5th/6th century AD and 11th/12th century AD, its component elements being putative Kshatriyas and mostly Brahmins, according to André Wink. (Wink, 1991)

Boses are considered as Kulin Kayasthas of Gautam gotra, along with Ghoshes, Mitras and Guhas.

2.4 Origins of the Bose Family of Ulpur

The Bose family of Ulpur were part of the Kayastha community said to have migrated to Bengal from Kannauj. One early leader of this clan was Pratapaditya, who rebelled against the Mughal emperor Akbar. He was defeated by Akbar's general Man Singh and forced to flee. His cousin Gopal Basu became a distinguished scholar in Banaras. Another prominent figure was Raghunandan Basu, who was granted a jagir or piece of land called Shahpur by the Mughal emperor Jahangir in exchange for an annual tribute. This was conferred as a do hazari, a grant rated at the service of 2,000 horseme. a mark of significant standing in the Mughal hierarchy.

Ulpur was founded by the Bose family as the central seat of their Jagir and came to be known as Shahpur Pargana. The pargana comprised 27 maujas (a village together with its surrounding farmlands, lakes, and greens) and had a population of 30,200 as recorded in the 1931 census. During the British period, the family became Zamindars or landlords, a status they held until independence and the subsequent abolition of zamindari in 1947.

The village of Ulpur in its heydays was the center of the district and had an active cultural life, along with a number of heritage buildings and a kali temple which still stands.

From the Wikipedia article on Ulpur and ulpur.org website:

"Dasarath Basu arrived in the 11th century in Bengal's Rarh region of present day West Bengal. One of his descendants, Raghunandan Basu, was reconfirmed the Zamindari/Jagir of

Ulpur/Shahpur by the Moghuls (Jahangir) in the 16th century, where his descendants settled. Many members of the Basu Roy Chowdhury clan of Ulpur left their ancestral home in East Bengal (now Bangladesh) after India was divided in 1947. However a few have remained behind and continue to participate in the social, political and cultural life of the area."

The title is passed on to all the sons. The title was kept as a name after the partition (1947 East Bengal became part of Pakistan and the family lost their estate) and the actual name Basu was dropped (Basu Roy Chowdhury of Ulpur). The family got another title, Thakur, which they stopped using once they lived in Ulpur (17th century). Roy is a Hindu title, which noblemen and those of royal blood took or were given. Chowdhury is a Mogul title, which the Mogul emperors gave to our ancestors for being their Jagirdars. Hence all the three elements – Thakur, Roy and Chowdhury are titles but given at different times, for different reasons.

The title Thakur, which the family held from the 17th century but stopped using once they settled in Ulpur, was dropped after Partition, as was the original surname Basu (the family being known thereafter simply as Roy Chowdhury or Bose). Roy is a Hindu title associated with nobility and royal lineage. Chowdhury is a Mughal title conferred upon our ancestors for their role as jagirdars. Thus, all three elements, Thakur, Roy, and Chowdhury, are honorary titles, each granted at a different time and for different reasons.

Faridpur has long been notable for its rich zamindari heritage. Among the prominent zamindar families of the district were the Basu Roys of Gopalganj, the Basu Roy Chowdhurys of Ulpur

(Shahpur), the Sikdars of Kanaipur, the Bhawal Rajas of Pangsha, and the Senguptas of Dhamaron, alongside several Muslim zamindari estates including the Chanpur Estate and the Boalmari Estate.

2.5 Ulpur Sammelani organization

The Ulpur Sammelani is a Kolkata based cultural organization of members of the Basu Roy Chowdhury family. They have an office address and regular meetings.

The address is as follows: Ulpur Sammelani charity foundation: Ulpur Sammilani 21/1, Central Park, Flat B-2, Kolkata 700 032 Tel: 2425 4348. Website: ulpur.org

References:

https://en.wikipedia.org/wiki/Charyapada

https://en.banglapedia.org/index.php/Bangali_Culture

https://en.wikipedia.org/wiki/Bose_(surname)

https://en.wikipedia.org/wiki/Bengali_Kayastha

Sengupta, Nitish K. (2001), History of the Bengali-Speaking People, UBS Publishers' Distributors.

Luca, P., Sarmila, B., Qasim, A., & Chris, T. (2017). Kayasthas of Bengal: Legends, Genealogies, and Genetics. Economic and Political Weekly, 52.

Akhtar, S. (1973). The role of the Zamindars in Bengal (1707-1772). University of London, School of Oriental and African Studies (United Kingdom).

Wikipedia. Ulpur. URL: https://en.wikipedia.org/wiki/Ulpur

Ulpur. URL: https://alchetron.com/Ulpur

https://wikimili.com/en/Ulpur

Andre Wink (1991). Al-Hind, the Making of the Indo-Islamic World, Volume 1. Brill Academic Publishers. p. 269. ISBN 978-90-04-09509-0. Retrieved 3 September 2011.

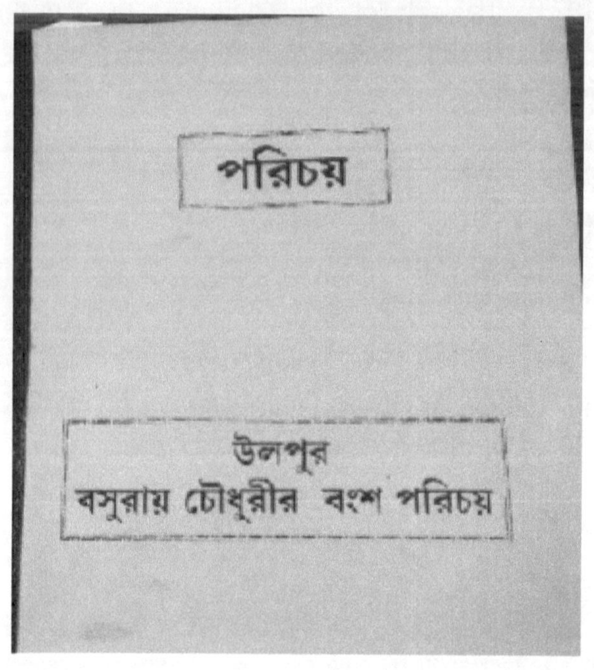

Figure: Cover of the book describing the family of Basu Roy Chowdhury

Figure: Geneological table of Bose family, taken from http://empireslastcasualty.blogspot.com/2008/02/ulpur-gopalganj-faridpur-district.html

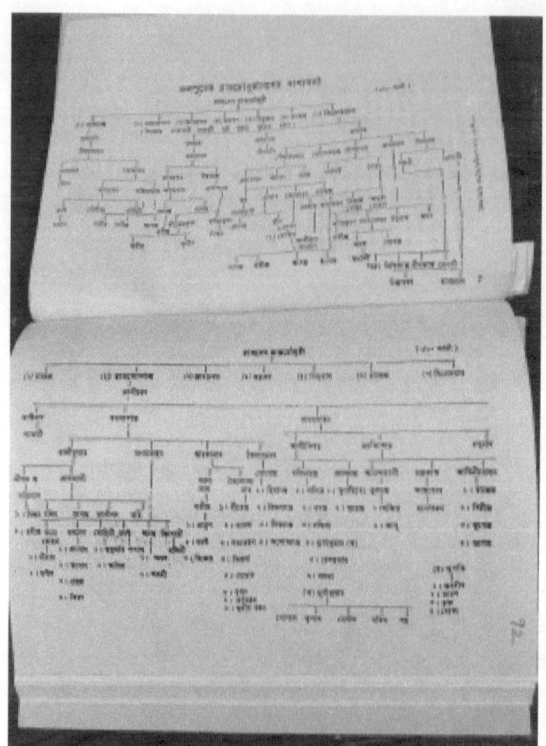

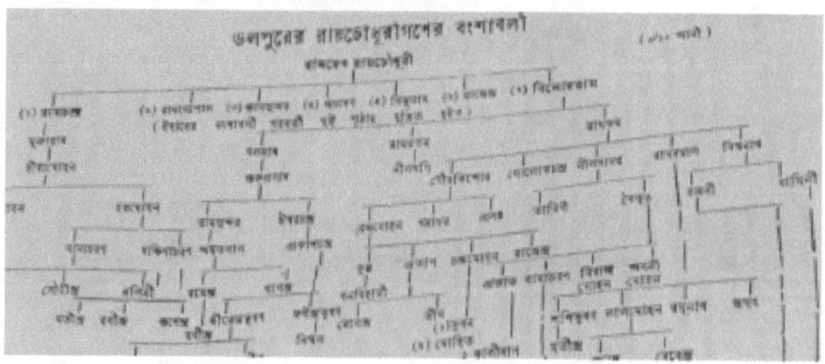

Figure: Geneological table of Bose family, taken from http://empireslastcasualty.blogspot.com/2008/02/ulpur-gopalganj-faridpur-district.html

Chapter 3: Zamindari Bari, Ancestral Home of the Bose Family

In this chapter, we briefly look at the ancestral house or Zamindari Bari of the Bose family of Ulpur.

3.1 How to get to Ulpur

Originally, the village of Ulpur was part of the Greater Faridpur district, but later it was moved to Gopalganj district in present day Bangladesh. It is located on the Gopalganj – Takerhat highway. The nearest town is Gopalganj. Ulpur is close to Gopalganj Sadar, about 10 km distance.

Ulpur is located about 140 km away from Dhaka via Mawa Ferry Ghat or the newly opened Padma toll bridge expressway.

The complete address is as follows: Ulpur Jomidar Bari, Village: Ulpur, Upazila: Gopalganj Sadar, District: Gopalganj, Country: Bangladesh.

One can search for "Ulpur" or "Ulpur bridge" or "Ulpur Zomidar Bari" on google maps and use the "directions" feature of google maps to find the exact directions, if one is traveling by car.

From Dhaka, one can get to Gopalganj using the bus, train or car. It is possible to do a day trip by car from Dhaka to Gopalganj and Ulpur, since the new Padma toll bridge expressway cuts the time of travel significantly to 3 to 4 hours.

- The bus is known as Tungipara express. It takes around 7 hours to cover the 200 km from Dhaka and AC bus and non-AC both are available. One can book the bus tickets online using Shohoz https://www.shohoz.com/bus-tickets/dhaka-to-gopalganj.
- If one wishes to take a car from Dhaka, it is a 3–4-hour drive by car via the newly opened Padma toll bridge expressway or 6 hours via the Dhaka-Khulna Highway.
- There is also a rail line by which one can get to Gopalganj from Dhaka on the Rajbari to Tungipara via Gopalganj city railway line.

From the Gopalganj town Kuadanga bus stand, one can take a bus to Ulpur bus stand which is 8-10 km, then hire a rickshaw to look at the old monuments of Ulpur Zamindari Bari. Or else, one can get to Gopalganj Sadar from Gopalganj city, from where one can take an electric or CNG autorickshaw to Ulpur which is around 8-10 km. It is also better to ask the people and the rickshaw pullers around where is Ulpur, once one reaches Gopalganj Sadar.

The village of Ulpur has a history of almost 500 years. Zamindari Bari, or landlord's estate, was a cluster of buildings which is among the prominent buildings of Ulpur. However, the buildings of the Zamindari bari have fallen into disuse since the past few decades. One can see the old heritage buildings soon after crossing the Ulpur bridge across Kaliganga river, and after driving to Ulpur Bazaar.

It is located off the main road, just after Ulpur Bridge on Kaliganga river is crossed.

Figure: Crossing Ulpur bridge on Kaliganga river by car

3.2 Route to Ulpur Zomidar Bari by car from Gopalganj Sadar Upazila

The route from Gopalganj Sadar to Ulpur Zomidar Bari ruins, as per Google maps, is as follows:

From Gopalganj Sadar Upazila, Bangladesh to Ulpur jomodar bari ruins 23 min (10.1 km) via R850 and Ulpur Bridge

Gopalganj Sadar Upazila, Bangladesh

Continue to Bangabandhu Rd/Gopalganj Town Rd/R850

6 min (1.3 km)

Follow R850 to Ulpur Bridge

18 min (8.4 km)

Continue on Ulpur Bridge to your destination

2 min (500 m)

Ulpur jomodar bari ruins,

Ulpur Jomodar Bari Ruins, Ulpur Bridge, Bangladesh

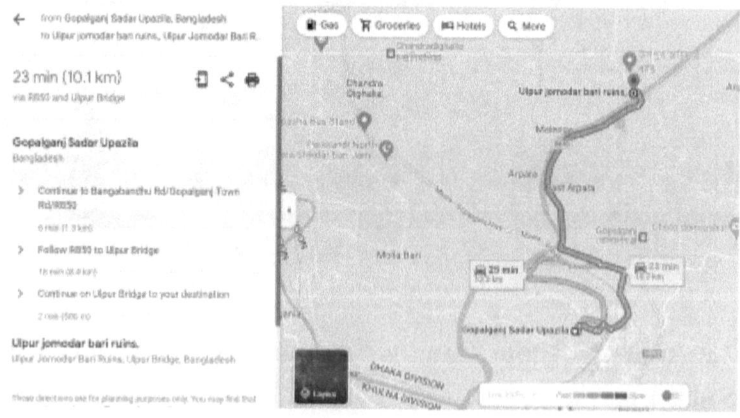

Figure: Screenshot of Google maps showing the route by car from Gopalganj Sadar Upazila to Ulpur Zomidar Bari ruins, via Ulpur Bridge

3.3 Nearby hotels to stay in Gopalganj

There are no hotels to stay in Ulpur village. However, there are some hotels in Gopalganj which is the nearest town.

In Gopalganj one can stay in some hotels overnight including Hotel Jimmy (01747-668405), Hotel Raj (01703-470240), Sohag Hotel (01787-504747). One can also taste the famous Dutt's sweets including Roshogolla.

3.4 Main Zomidar Bari Buildings Surviving in Ulpur

At its height, the Ulpur Zamindari estate comprised more than 100 buildings constructed by successive zamindars of the Bose family. In the early 1900s, Zamindar Pritish Chandra Roy Chowdhury built the centrepiece of the estate, a grand residential complex on 200 acres of land. This became the main Ulpur Zamindari Bari.

After Partition, the patriarch of the family moved to Kolkata, and the new government took possession of the land. Several of the Zamindari Bari buildings were converted to government offices, including the Tehsil office in Gopalganj Sadar Upazila, the Union Land Office, the Sub Post Office, and the Upazila Registry Office. The Bangladesh Archaeological Conservation Department is engaged in efforts to preserve some of the heritage monuments. Other buildings are now used as residences by villagers, or for storing grain.

The village of Ulpur has a history of almost 500 years. One well-dressed local resident, when asked for directions, told a visitor: 'Go visit your home that we call the 19 Judges Home, as there were 19 judges from that family during the British Raj era' — an indication of the lasting impression the family left on the local community.

The main surviving structures include:

- **Dinesh Dham (Sub Post Office)**: A two-storey residential building, still in active use as the local post office.
- **Din Dham (Upazila Land Registry Office)**: A two-storey building close to the main road, now disused since a new Land Registry office was built adjacent to it. Occasionally used by villagers for storing fodder.
- **19 Judges Home (Unishta Judger Bari)**: Located further into Ulpur village; named for the remarkable number of judges the family produced during the British Raj.
- **Kali Temple**: An old temple to Goddess Kali, currently unused but recently repainted.
- **New Museum Complex**: Built by the local government on the site of the Jomidar Bari, including a multi-storey museum dedicated to Bangabandhu Sheikh Mujibur Rahman (who was born in nearby Tungipara), a new Kali temple, a samadhi dedicated to the patriarch Sudhanya Kumar Roy Chowdhury and his wife Anima Roy Chowdhury, and a lake with a walkway.

3.5 Land Registry Office Building in Ulpur (unused now)

The Upazila land registration office building is one of the surviving houses of the Ulpur Zomidar Bari. It is a two-storey structure situated just off the main road after crossing Ulpur Bridge. It has been disused since a new land registration office was constructed immediately adjacent to it, and it is now gradually being reclaimed by vegetation. Despite its neglected state, the building's ornate arched windows and decorative façade reveal the refined architectural taste of its original builders.

Figure: Exterior of Ulpur Land Registry Office Building, off the main road after crossing Ulpur Bridge. Now defunct, once part of the Zamindari Bari.

Figure: Exterior of Ulpur Land Registry Office Building seen from the side. Now defunct, once part of the Zamindari Bari.

Figure: Exterior of Ulpur Land Registry Office Building seen from the back. Now defunct, once part of the Zamindari Bari.

Figure: Interiors of Ulpur Land Registry Office Building on ground floor. Now defunct, once part of the Zamindari Bari.

Figure: Interiors of Ulpur Land Registry Office Building on ground floor. Now defunct, once part of the Zamindari Bari.

Figure: Interiors of Ulpur Land Registry Office Building on ground floor. Now defunct, once part of the Zamindari Bari.

Figure: The new land registry office constructed just next to the old building

Figure: The author visiting the land registry office building in Ulpur. Now defunct, once part of the Zamindari Bari.

Figure: Varendah on first floor of the land registry office building. Now defunct, once part of the Zamindari Bari.

Figure: Varendah on first floor of the land registry office building. Now defunct, once part of the Zamindari Bari.

3.6 Village pond next to Kali temple and Post Office Building in Ulpur

Driving past the land registry office building and into Ulpur village, one arrives at Ulpur market. Adjacent to the market is an open space next to the village pond. From here, the post office building and the Kali temple are visible nearby, along with a few local shops. The scene is peaceful, the pond shaded by trees, with the old post office building rising behind it, a reminder of the estate's former grandeur.

The post office building is a two-storey structure, still in active use. It is perhaps the best-preserved of the original Zamindari Bari buildings, with its arched verandahs and decorated upper floor still largely intact. The Kali temple next to the pond has been recently repainted in bright colours and stands in good condition, though it appears to be unused for regular worship.

Figure: Village pond, close to the post office and kali temple and shops

3.6 Post Office Building in Ulpur (still in use)

The post office building is still in use and is a two storied residential building, part of the Ulpur Zomidar Bari.

Figure: Front of the Post office building. Once part of the Zamindari bari.

Figure: Post office building, along with a couple of other buildings

Figure: A closer view of the Post office building, once part of Zamindari bari

Figure: Side and back view of the Post office building, once part of Zamindari bari

Figure: The author in front of the Post office building

3.7 Kali temple

There is an empty kali temple next to the village pond and opposite the post office building. It is brightly painted recently.

Figure: Kali temple beside the village pond, close to the Post office building

3.7 Road to the village past the Kali temple and pond

A path leads further into the village past the kali temple and the village pond. We pass through some residential houses and a school on the left.

Figure: Road leading into the village from the Kali temple and past the pond

3.8 Ulpur Zomidar bari new building and museum

A brick-paved path leads further into the village, past the Kali temple and the pond, through residential houses and past a school. Eventually one arrives at the gate of the new Ulpur Zomidar Bari museum complex, built by the local government. This complex includes:

A multi-storey museum dedicated to Bangabandhu Sheikh Mujibur Rahman, featuring photographs and quotes from his life.

The Mujib Gallery, an open-air display of large photographic panels.

A new Kali temple, ornately decorated, with lion statues guarding the entrance.

A two-storey building displaying portraits of the late patriarch of the Basu Roy Chowdhury family, Sudhanya Kumar Roy Chowdhury, and his wife Anima Roy Chowdhury.

A memorial samadhi (cenotaph) dedicated to the patriarch and his wife, decorated in traditional temple style with their portraits.

A scenic lake with a walkway and seating areas.

It is a mark of respect that the local government has chosen to memorialize both the patriarchs of the Bose family and Bangabandhu on the same site, recognizing the historic importance of the location to the region's past.

Figure: Multi Floor Museum dedicated to Bangabandhu Sheikh Mujibur Rahman

Figure: Bangabandhu Sheikh Mujib gallery

Figure: Two floor building with pictures of the patriarch of the Basu Roy Chowdhury family, Sudhanya Kumar Roy Chowdhury and his wife Anima Roy Chowdhury

Figure: Courtyard with two floor building and new kali temple

Figure: Front of the new kali temple

Figure: Picture of the late patriarch of the Basu Roy Chowdhury family, Sudhanya Kumar Roy Chowdhury

Figure: Picture of the late wife of the patriarch of the Basu Roy Chowdhury family, Anima Roy Chowdhury

Figure: Beautiful memorial to the late patriarch of the Bose Roy Chowdhury family and his wife

Figure: Beautiful lake with walkway behind the new kali temple

References:

https://en.banglapedia.org/
index.php?title=Gopalganj_Sadar_Upazila

Offroad Bangladesh. Ulpur Zamindar Bari. URL:
http://offroadbangladesh.com/places/ulpur-zamindar-bari/

The Financial Express, Oct 13 2020. Ulpur Zamindar House in Gopalganj in shabby state. URL: https://thefinancialexpress.com.bd/national/ulpur-zamindar-house-in-gopalganj-in-shabby-state-1602589494

Daily Asian Age, July 2017. The historical place at Gopalganj. URL: https://dailyasianage.com/news/70639/the-historical-place-at-gopalganj

A lonely traveler, August 2014. Gopalganj – Ulpur Jomidar Bari. https://www.alonelytraveler.com/gopalganj-ulpur-jomidar-bari/

Abid, Travel Bangladesh. Mar 23 2021. Famous Dutt's Sweets of Gopalganj. https://travelbd.xyz/en/famous-dutts-sweets-of-gopalganj

Archaeological survey report of Greater Faridpur District (2017), by Md. Abul Hashem Miah, Nazimuddin Ahmad, Bangladesh. Dept. of Archaeology

District Statistics 2011 Gopalganj, Bangladesh Bureau of Statistics (BBS).

Figure: Map of Gopalganj Sadar Upazila, taken from https://en.banglapedia.org/index.php/Gopalganj_Sadar_Upazila

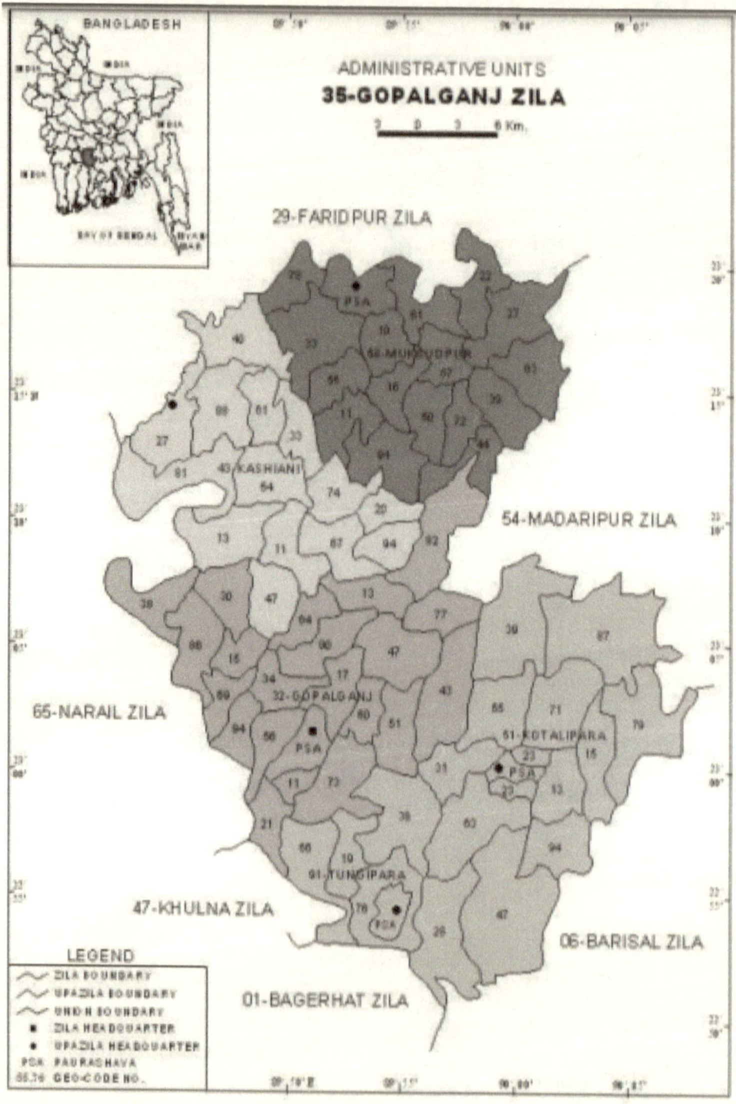

Figure: Map of Gopalganj district, of which Ulpur is a part. Taken from District Statistics 2011 Gopalganj, Bangladesh Bureau of Statistics (BBS).

Figure: Some landmarks in Ulpur, Taken from Google maps. The Ulpur Zamindari Bari is highlighted. Maps Data @ Google 2022

Figure: Ancestral home, Zamindari Bari of Basu Roy Chowdhury in Ulpur, Gopalganj. Taken from ulpur.org

Figure: One of the old buildings of the Zamindari Bari in Ulpur, converted to the post office which is still in use today. Taken from Google maps. Maps Data @ Google 2022

Figure: one of the walls from the old Zamindari Bari in Ulpur. Taken from http://offroadbangladesh.com/places/ulpur-zamindar-bari/

Figure: An old temple in Ulpur, previously part of the Zomidar Bari. Taken from Google maps. Maps Data @ Google 2022

Figure: Photo from inside one of the old buildings of the Zomidar (Zamindari) bari of Ulpur. Taken from Google maps. Maps Data @ Google 2022

Figure: One of the buildings in the Zamindari bari of Ulpur. Taken from Google maps. Maps Data @ Google 2022

Chapter 4: Bose Family after Partition of India

In this chapter, we briefly discuss the migration of the various branches of the Bose family after the partition of India.

4.1 Partition and its impact

The Partition of Bengal in 1947, the second such partition in the 20th century, the first having occurred under Lord Curzon in 1905, was one of the most traumatic events in the history of South Asia. The Radcliffe Line divided Bengal along religious lines, with the Muslim-majority east becoming East Pakistan (later Bangladesh in 1971), and the Hindu-majority west remaining as part of India.

Faridpur district, which had been part of the Bengal Presidency and contained Ulpur, was assigned to East Pakistan. This consigned the ancestral home of the Basu Roy Chowdhury family to a foreign country overnight. Like millions of other Bengali Hindus, the family were forced to abandon their lands, property, and centuries of roots, and start afresh in India. The displacement was sudden and the trauma profound. According to one estimate, millions of Hindus crossed westward into India from East Bengal in the years following Partition, most settling in West Bengal, with others dispersing to Delhi, Assam, Tripura, and beyond.

4.2 Branches of the Bose family of Ulpur

There were supposedly five branches of the Bose family. One of the branches of the family remained in Ulpur while most of the branches migrated to India, mostly to Kolkata but also some in Delhi and other cities of India. The patriarch of the family, Protosh Chandra Roy, moved to Kolkata after partition.

Recently, many members of the Bose family have also settled abroad such as in UK, USA and Europe.

Figure: Sarbari Roy Chowdhury

4.3 Famous Ulpurians: Sarbari Roy Chowdhury

A notable member of the Ulpur Bose family was Sarbari Roy Chowdhury, who was born in 1933 in Ulpur. He was a famous Bengali sculptor.

Sarbari Roy Chowdhury graduated from the Government College of Art and Craft, located in Calcutta, in 1956. He began working at the Indian Art College, Kolkata in the 1960s. In 1969 he joined the Kala Bhavan at Santiniketan Visva Bharati University, set up by Rabindranath Tagore and worked there as a member of the academic staff until his retirement in 1997. He died in 2012.

His work was in an innovative style that mixed sculptural elements from the east and west. He won several awards for his work, including Gagan-Abani Puraskar from Visva Bharati University, Santiniketan, in 2004, and the Abanindra Puraskar from the Government of West Bengal in 2005.

Figure: Subrata Roy Chowdhury

4.4 Famous Ulpurians: Subrata Roy Chowdhury

Another famous Ulpurian was Subrata Roy Chowdhury. He was a lawyer in the Calcutta High Court and also the Supreme Court of India. He was an activist in the area of international human rights law. He published a book about the 9 months liberation war of Bangladesh. He also helped draft the proclamation of independence of Bangladesh in 1971.

4.5 Famous personalities from Gopalganj district

The district Gopalganj, of which Ulpur is currently a part, has also given rise to many prominent personalities. Chief among them is Bangabandhu Sheikh Mujibur Rahman, the first president of Bangladesh, who came from village Tungipara in Gopalganj district. Same goes for his daughter, the former Prime Minister of Bangladesh, Sheikh Hasina Wajed.

Chapter 5: Bose Family in Delhi

In this chapter, we briefly go through the history of Bengalis in Delhi and specifically about our Bose family who settled in Delhi.

5.1 Bengalis in Delhi

Bengalis in Delhi have existed since the Mughal times. However, their population grew significantly after the capital of India was shifted by the British from Kolkata to Delhi in 1911, and many Bengali government servants from Kolkata migrated to Delhi to work in newly constructed central government offices in New Delhi.

Figure: Exterior of New Delhi Kalibari in Mandir Marg.

Most of the new Bengalis settled in areas of old Delhi (North Delhi) in the 20th century such as Kashmere Gate, Tis Hazari, Gol Market, Minto Road and also RK Puram. The oldest of the Kali mandirs and Durga Pujas in Delhi are around the same locations. For example, Kashmere Gate Durga Puja is the oldest Durga Puja in Delhi and has been running since 1910.

Cultural institutions like the Bengali club in Kashmere Gate and schools like the Bengali Boys' School were formed in early 20th century, to cater to the middle class Bengali community in Delhi.

5.2 Settling of Bose Family in Kashmere Gate

After partition, our branch of the Bose family settled as a joint family in the Kashmere gate area in Old Delhi, where already many Bengalis were staying. It was close to the Delhi College of Engineering whose original campus was in Kashmere Gate.

The boys went to a Bengali medium school called Bengali Boys Senior Secondary School, nowadays called "Bengali Senior Secondary School", located near Kashmere Gate. The girls went to different colleges of the Delhi University.

There was a social club called Bengali club in Kashmere Gate which they used to frequent and which had some sports, library, reading room and recreation facilities. The Bengali Club was founded in 1925 and was the oldest Bengali club in Delhi. It lies on the first floor of a heritage building and was restored and reopened in 2016 with the help in restoration given by the Delhi chapter of INTACH.

Figure: Exterior of the Bengali Club building in Kashmere Gate (taken from https://www.hindustantimes.com/art-and-culture/delhi-s-oldest-bengali-club-is-back-in-action/story-2SalHAbN1OwUF2mGSo52RL.html)

Figure: Interior of the Bengali Club building in Kashmere Gate (taken from https://www.hindustantimes.com/art-and-culture/delhi-s-oldest-bengali-club-is-back-in-action/story-2SalHAbN1OwUF2mGSo52RL.html)

Figure: Building of the Bengali senior Secondary School in Kashmere Gate, also site of the Kashmere Gate Durga Puja

Figure: Inside of the Bengali senior Secondary School in Kashmere Gate, also site of the Kashmere Gate Durga Puja

The Bose family also used to be regular patrons of the Durga Puja in Kashmere Gate, which was one of the earliest Durga Pujas in Delhi with a history of more than 100 years. They used to help out with arranging the snacks and distributing them with the coupons, and also things like cutting the fruits and vegetables for the puja to the Goddess.

Figure: Priest performing the arati of Goddess Durga at Kashmere gate Durga puja, at the site of the Bengali Boys School

5.3 Brief history of Chittaranjan Park Bengali colony in Delhi

The partition brought many Hindu Bengalis from East Bengal or East Pakistan (later Bangladesh after 1972), including the Bose family, to Delhi. Many of the new Bengalis immigrants originally settled in Kashmere Gate and other areas in Old Delhi such as Minto Road and Gole Market, where Bengalis were already residing earlier. The East Bengal Displaced Persons (EBDP) Association was formed in 1954 to support and take care of the displaced persons of the partition.

The Indian government in early 1960s allocated a parcel of land to the Bengalis in what was originally a forested and rocky area. The original allotees were given plots of land upon showing some proof of their property in East Bengal. After that, many of the new refugees moved to that location.

For reference, a similar plot of land was also given by the Indian government to Hindu Punjabis who came from West Punjab to Delhi after the partition and was named Lajpat Nagar after the freedom fighter Lala Lajpat Rai.

The Bengali colony was originally called EPDP colony (East Pakistan Displaced Persons Colony) and Purbachal and later renamed as Chittaranjan Park (CR Park for short) after the respected freedom fighter Deshbandhu Chittaranjan Das.

The Delhi Development Authority or DDA also helped in constructing many of the original houses in CR Park, as well as building a separate residential colony in nearby Kalkaji.

Soon the forested and rocky areas of CR Park developed into a residential colony, complete with a Kali temple on top of the hill, cultural institutions such as Bangiya Samaj, East Bengal Displaced Persons (EBDP) Association, Chittaranjan memorial society and markets where one could buy Bengali food and other supplies.

Nowadays, CR Park is considered an affluent and upscale colony in South Delhi. Due to rise in house prices generally and especially in South Delhi, getting a flat here for rent or buying is relatively expensive.

5.4 Settling of Bose Family in Chittaranjan Park

Our branch of the Bose family, similar to many other Bengali families who had migrated from East Bengal, eventually obtained a parcel of land in CR Park around 1968 from the Delhi government, constructed a house on the plot of land, initially giving it for rent and finally moved from Kashmere Gate to the house in CR Park around the early 2000s.

References:

Nikita Saxena, Hindustan Times, May 14 22016. Delhi's oldest Bengali club is back in action. https://www.hindustantimes.com/art-and-culture/delhi-s-oldest-bengali-club-is-back-in-action/story-2SalHAbN1OwUF2mGSo52RL.html

East Bengal Displaced Persons Association http://ebdp.weebly.com/

Chittaranjan Park Bangiya Samaj https://bangiyasamaj.org/

Deshbandhu Chittaranjan Memorial Society https://chittaranjanbhawan.com/

Bengali Senior Secondary School Kashmiri Gate Delhi https://www.facebook.com/bengaliseniorsecondaryschooldelhi/

Chapter 6: The Story of an Unselfish Lady

In this chapter, we narrate a personal story about our branch of the Bose family that settled in Delhi. It is the story of a person, a member of our Bose family, who sacrificed a lot to make sure her big family was well settled.

When our Bose family arrived in Delhi in the 1940s, away from the ravages of the partition of their Bengal homeland, they had little money. They had lost their ancestral land in Ulpur and now had very little money, except for some land deeds and a hope to find some government job in Delhi. It was a large family, with three young boys and five girls. The boys were still young, around 6 to 12 years of age when they first arrived in Delhi, and the girls were only slightly older.

It was just after independence in India and there was a lot of scarcity. One of the few ways to rise above the scarcity was through education. But getting a good education too was not easy and needed money.

The family initially manage to get a living place in an area in Mori gate called Gandha Nala market, where there were a few other Bengali families, and later in Kashmere Gate in North Delhi, also home to a population of Bengalis in those decades.

In these circumstances one of the elder sisters took the responsibility for her large family, whose name was Lipika Bose.

While her father was mainly working to gain a meagre salary to afford food and other necessities for the family, and her mother was busy cooking and taking care of the children, she took it upon herself to raise her young brothers and arranging their education and helping them to get jobs.

Figure: Lipika Bose in her old age

Lipika graduated from Delhi University with a bachelors in English and soon afterwards found a job as an English lecturer in a college near Delhi. She would commute all the way from Delhi to Meerut on the bus and back. In those days, which were in the 1950s and 1960s, it was difficult enough for a young woman to travel and teach. However, Lipika managed to save enough money to pay for her brothers' school fees in Bengali

Boys school in Kashmere Gate, and soon afterwards also the college fees. Later, she got a job in Shyama Prasad Mukherji College of the Delhi University in Punjabi Bagh, as a reader (associate professor) of English.

Lipika soon managed to fund the complete school education of her three brothers. She also funded the university education of the brothers with her savings. However, all this came at the cost of her personal life, and she elected to remain unmarried to devote her full time to her brothers' education, helping her mother and other family responsibilities. Funding the full-time education from school fees all the way to university graduation of three boys in those times was no mean achievement.

Figure: House in Kashmere Gate where the Bose family stayed for 40 years before moving to CR Park

Soon, the family moved to slightly better quarters in the top floor of Bedi Bhavan in Kashmere Gate. They lived as a joint family, as was common in those days.

Meanwhile, the other sisters, namely Eva, Reva, Kathika, and Monika too completed their graduate education and got jobs and married, while Lipika remained unmarried. Eva got a government job in the telephone department, Reva became a doctor although she unfortunately died at a young age, Kathika was a housewife and provided home tuition to some kids in the locality, and Monika opened a highly successful sweets shop called Annapurna Sweet House in Chittaranjan Park.

When the government of India in 1970s announced the giving of plots of land in a new colony for Bengalis and Punjabis who had escaped from the partition, Lipika applied and obtained a plot in the forested area called EPDP colony and later to be named Chittaranjan Park. In this plot she built a house of three floors for the three brothers, all from her own savings and also assisting her mother to take care of the whole family upon the unfortunate demise of her father.

Eventually, the house on the plot in Chittaranjan Park was ready and Lipika moved in with the family. Some of the brothers had already married and moved out by then, including the middle brother, Kali Prasad, who got a job in Mumbai/Bombay in a fertilizer company and the youngest brother, Siva Prasad, one of the authors of this book, who got an engineering degree from Jadavpur University in Kolkata and a job in Uttar Pradesh State Electricity Board. The eldest brother, Deva Prasad, stayed with the joint family and also shared some of the responsibilities, despite being hurt at an unfortunate accident and losing half a leg. The other sisters in the family also eventually got houses near Chittaranjan Park.

All her life, Lipika dedicated herself to serving her family and take care of her three brothers to help complete their education and get employment. Ultimately in 2015 Lipika died, surrounded by her extended family, in a hospital close to the house she had built, having achieved her goal of caring for the whole family and especially making the three brothers stand on their own feet and get married with their own families, and soon after a couple of her brothers' kids also got married.

This is the story of Lipika, a person who did everything to make sure the Bose family could thrive in the new and unfamiliar environment of Delhi, in the midst of all the difficulties. Her sacrifices ensured the stability and success of the Bose family.

Chapter 7: Conclusion

In this book, we have traced the history and journey of the Basu Roy Chowdhury family, also known as the Bose family, from their ancestral roots in Ulpur, Faridpur district, through the upheaval of the Partition of 1947, to their resettlement in India and beyond.

Through historical research, genealogical records, personal memories, and an on-the-ground visit to the ancestral home, we have attempted to reconstruct a picture of our family's long past. From the days of being jagirdars under the Mughal empire, when Raghunandan Basu received the Shahpur Pargana as a do hazari jagir from Emperor Jahangir, to the role of Zamindars during the British era, and then to the trials of displacement and the painstaking rebuilding of lives in Delhi, our family's resilience is evident at every stage of this story.

The ancestral home at Ulpur, though now largely in ruins, continues to stand as a testament to the family's history. Some buildings have been repurposed as government offices; others are slowly being reclaimed by vegetation. The local government's decision to build a new museum complex on the estate grounds, and to include memorials to the patriarch of the Basu Roy Chowdhury family alongside a tribute to Bangabandhu Sheikh Mujibur Rahman, ensures that the site retains its significance for the region.

The timeline added to this edition offers a chronological overview that places the family's story within the broader sweep of Bengali and South Asian history, from the Mughal era, through British colonial rule, through Partition, and into the present day.

It is our hope that this book serves not only as a personal family archive but as a contribution to the larger narrative of South Asian history, particularly of those families affected by the Partition and the diaspora experience. We also hope it preserves a legacy for future generations of the family, wherever in the world they may now be.

The journey of the Bose family continues, carried forward by descendants across India and the world. We dedicate this book to all of them, with gratitude and hope.

About the Authors

Siva Prasad Bose is an author of various introductory guidebooks related to aspects of Indian laws. He is currently retired after many years of service in Uttar Pradesh Power Corporation Limited. He received his engineering degree from Jadavpur University, Kolkata and has a law degree from Meerut University, Meerut and a BSc from MMH College Ghaziabad. His interests lie in the fields of family law, civil law, law of contracts, and areas of law related to power electricity related issues.

Joy Bose is a data scientist and researcher.

Other Books by Siva Prasad Bose

Introduction to Wills and Probate

Senior Citizens Abuse in India

Introduction to Negotiable Instruments

Introduction to Marriage Laws in India

Neighbor Problems in India and what to do about them

Managing Court Cases with Mental Strength

Delays in Court Cases in India

Self-Publish Books and E-Books in India

Introduction to Patents and Patent Law in India

Introduction to Property Law in India

Did you love *The Bose Family of Faridpur*? Then you should read *A Walk in Chittaranjan Park*[1] by Siva Prasad Bose and Joy Bose!

[2]

Chittaranjan Park or CR park is a residential colony in South Delhi, bordered by Greater Kailash 1 and 2 and located close to areas such as Nehru place, Alaknanda, Kalkaji and Govindpuri. It is sometimes called "Little Kolkata" because of the Kolkata style street food, Bengali culture and festivals celebrated here.

Previously called EPDP Colony or East Pakistan Displaced Persons Colony and Purbachal, CR Park is a Bengali dominated colony that was originally developed to house refugees of partition from East Bengal, but has recently become more

1. https://books2read.com/u/bMYWXv

2. https://books2read.com/u/bMYWXv

diverse. It is a cultural treat famous for its celebration of Durga Puja, Bengali snacks and sweets.

In this book we discuss the famous landmarks and festivals in CR Park. This is intended to be partly a travel guide for those who want to experience this microcosm of Bengali culture in New Delhi.

Our own Bose family has been resident in Delhi for a very long time, originally residing in Kashmere Gate and later moving to CR Park.

About the Author

Siva Prasad Bose is an electrical engineer by profession. He is currently retired after many years of service in Uttar Pradesh Power Corporation Limited. He received his engineering degree from Jadavpur University, Kolkata and has a law degree from Meerut University, Meerut. His interests lie in the fields of family law, civil law, law of contracts, and any areas of law related to power electricity related issues.

Read more at https://sivaprasadbose.wordpress.com/.